First paperback edition 2021
Book design by Lin & Edwin Choi
ISBN 979-8-6676-5208-3

For a free audiobook version, please visit:

www.linwinbooks.com

For our son Ethan:

may you have the world

Dim Sum, Please!
我要點心!
(ngo5 jiu3 dim2 sam1)

Written by: Lin and Edwin Choi

www.linwinbooks.com

Dim sum is usually eaten in the morning.
Dim sum consists of many small delicious dishes
eaten with tea. I am going to order some of
the most popular dishes for you to try.
點心通常早上食. 點心係好多小碟配茶.
我點最出名嘅碟畀你試吓.
(dim2 sam1 tung1 soeng4 zou2 soeng6 sik6.
dim2 sam1 hai6 hou2 do1 siu2 dip6 pui3
caa4. ngo5 dim2 zeoi3 ceot1 ming4 ge3
dip6 bei2 nei5 si3 haa5)

Shrimp dumplings, shrimp dumplings,
Shrimp dumplings are so yummy!
蝦餃, 蝦餃, 蝦餃好食!
(haa1 gaau2, haa1 gaau2,
haa1 gaau2 hou2 sik6!)

Shrimp
蝦
(haa1)

Bamboo shoots
竹筍
(zuk1 seon2)

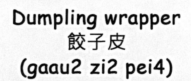

Dumpling wrapper
餃子皮
(gaau2 zi2 pei4)

Shrimp dumplings
蝦餃
(haa1gaau2)

Soy sauce
豉油
(si6 jau4)

Oil
油
(jau2)

Star anise
八角
(baat3 gok3)

Chicken feet
雞腳
(gai1 goek3)

Phoenix claws
鳳爪
(fung6 zaau2)

Flour
麵粉
(min6 fan2)

Egg
雞蛋
(gai1 daan2)

Sugar
糖
(tong4)

Butter
牛油
(ngau4 jau4)

Egg tart
蛋撻
(daan6 taat1)

BBQ pork buns, BBQ pork buns,
BBQ pork buns are delicious!
叉燒包, 叉燒包, 叉燒包好正!
(caa1 siu1 baau1, caa1 siu1 baau1,
caa1 siu1 baau1 hou2 zeng3!)

Shumai wrapper
舒迈皮
(syu1 maai6 pei4)

Shrimp
蝦
(haa1)

Mushrooms
蘑菇
(mo4 gu1)

Pork
豬肉
(zyu1 juk6)

Shumai
燒賣
(siu1 maai6)

Soy sauce
豉油
(si6 jau4)

Flour
麵粉
(min6 fan2)

Roasted pork
叉燒
(caa1 siu1)

BBQ pork bun
叉燒包
(caa1 siu1 baau1)

Beef
牛肉
(ngau4 juk6)

Rice flour
米粉
(mai5 fan2)

Soy sauce
豉油
(si6 jau4)

Rice noodle roll
腸粉
(coeng2 fan2)

Chicken
雞
(gai1)

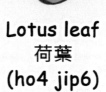

Lotus leaf
荷葉
(ho4 jip6)

Chinese sausage
臘腸
(laap6 coeng4)

Mushrooms
蘑菇
(mo4 gu1)

Sticky rice
糯米雞
(no6 mai5 gai1)

Rice flour
米粉
(mai5 fan2)

Dried shrimp
蝦米
(haa1 mai5)

Turnip
蘿蔔
(lo4 baak6)

Chinese sausage
臘腸
(laap6 coeng4)

Turnip cake
蘿蔔糕
(lo4 baak6 gou1)

Cantonese pronunciation is typically practiced with the two most common Latin letter styles: Yale and Jyutping. Both are listed below. For a full pronunciation guide, please proceed to https://lifeofl.in/cantonese and use this chart as a reference.

Tones

Kisa/IPA	Lau	Yale	Jyutping	CPB
˥	1, °	à, ā	1	à
˧˥	2, *	á	2	á
˧	3	a	3	ā
˨˩	4	àh	4	a
˩˧	5	áh	5	á
˨	6	ah	6	ā

Finals

Kisa	IPA	Lau	Yale	Jyutping	CPB
a	aː	a	a	aa	a
ai	aːi	aai	aai	aai	aai
au	aːu	aau	aau	aau	aau
am	am	aam	aam	aam	aam
an	an	aan	aap	aan	aan
ang	aŋ	aang	aang	aang	aang
ap	apˋ	aap	aap	aap	aap
at	atˋ	aat	aat	aat	aat
ak	akˋ	aak	aak	aak	aak

Kisa	IPA	Lau	Yale	Jyutping	CPB
ɐi	ɐi	ai	ai	ai	ai
ɐu	ɐu	au	au	au	au
ɐm	ɐ	am	am	am	am
ɐn	ɐn	an	an	an	an
ɐng	ɐŋ	ang	ang	ang	ang
ɐp	ɐpˋ	ap	ap	ap	ap
ɐt	ɐtˋ	at	at	at	at
ɐk	ɐkˋ	ak	ak	ak	ak

Kisa	IPA	Lau	Yale	Jyutping	CPB
o	ɔː	oh	o	o	oh
oi	ɔːi	oi	oi	oi	oi
ou	ou	o	ou	ou	o
on	ɔn	on	on	on	on
ong	ɔŋ	ong	ong	ong	ong
ot	ɔtˋ	ot	ot	ot	ot
ok	ɔkˋ	ok	ok	ok	ok

Kisa	IPA	Lau	Yale	Jyutping	CPB
e	ɛː	e	e	e	e
ei	ei	ei	ei	ei	ei
eu	ɛːu			eu	
eng	ɛŋ	eng	eng	eng	eng

Initials

Kisa	IPA	Lau	Yale	Jyutping	CPB
b	p	b	b	b	b
p	pʰ	p	p	p	p
m	m	m	m	m	m
f	f	f	f	f	f
d	t	d	d	d	d
t	tʰ	t	t	t	t
l	l	l	l	l	l
g	k	g	g	g	g
k	kʰ	k	k	k	k
h	h	h	h	h	h
dz	ts	j	j	z	j
ts	tsʰ	ch	ch	c	ch
s	s	s	s	s	s
y	j	y	y	j	y
w	w	w	w	w	w
gw	kʷ	gw	gw	gw	gw
kw	kʷʰ	kw	kw	kw	kw

Kisa	IPA	Lau	Yale	Jyutping	CPB
ɛk	ɛkˋ	ek	ek	ek	ek

Kisa	IPA	Lau	Yale	Jyutping	CPB
i	iː	i	i	i	i
iu	iːu	iu	iu	iu	iu
im	im	im	im	im	im
in	in	in	in	in	in
Ing	ɪŋ	ing	ing	ing	ing
ip	ipˋ	ip	ip	ip	ip
it	itˋ	it	it	it	it
Ik	ɪkˋ	ik	ik	ik	ik

Kisa	IPA	Lau	Yale	Jyutping	CPB
œ	oeː	euh	eu	oe	euh
öü	əy	ui	eui	eoi	ui
ön	ən	un	eun	eon	un
œng	oeŋ	eung	eung	oeng	eung
öt	ətˋ	ut	eut	eot	ut
œk	oekˋ	euk	euk	oek	euk

Kisa	IPA	Lau	Yale	Jyutping	CPB
u	uː	oo	u	u	oo
ui	uːi	ooi	ui	ui	ooi
un	un	oon	un	un	oon
Ung	ʊŋ	ung	ung	ung	ung
ut	utˋ	oot	ut	ut	oot
Uk	ʊkˋ	uk	uk	uk	uk

Kisa	IPA	Lau	Yale	Jyutping	CPB
ü	yː	ue	yu	yu	ue
ün	yn	uen	yun	yun	uen
üt	ytˋ	uet	yut	yut	uet

Kisa	IPA	Lau	Yale	Jyutping	CPB
m	m	m	m	m	m
ng	ŋ	ng	ng	ng	ng

Here's a quick guide to the six Cantonese tones in Jyutping order:

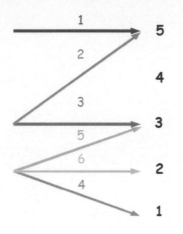

Diagram of Cantonese tones. The arrows are numbered to represent tones 1-6. Vocal range is marked vertically from owest (1) to highest (6).

Tone 1: High flat. Equivalent to the first tone in Mandarin.

Tone 2: Rising, like you're asking a question. Equivalent to second tone in Mandarin.

Tone 3: Flat mid-pitch, lower than first tone. Unique to Cantonese.

Tone 4: Low falling. Starts with low tone and drops. Similar to the Mandarin fourth tone.

Tone 5: Low rising. Similar to second tone in Mandarin, but lower.

Tone 6: Low level. Similar to third tone in Mandarin, but lower.